PHOTO BY WERNER J. KUHN

MONEY

A MUSICAL PLAY FOR CABARET

Book and Lyrics by
DAVID AXLEROD and TOM WHEDON

Music by **SAM POTTLE**

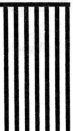

**DRAMATISTS
PLAY SERVICE
INC.**

"MONEY" was first presented at the Upstairs at the Downstairs, New York, on July 9, 1963, with the following cast:

HARRY CLAY ....David Rounds

CYNTHIA BURGESS ....Barbara Quaney

BERNIE BARTOK ....Jon Stone

MR. MANN ....George Coe

MUSICAL DIRECTOR ....Sam Pottle

AT THE PIANOS ....Sam Pottle
                                        Bob Rogers

Production Directed By
Ronny Graham

PRODUCTION NOTES

In the original production, two studio pianos were used. They were located u., facing the audience. A slit traveller curtain, allowing performers to poke their heads out from behind, was used in Act I scene 2, in the beginning of scene 4, and throughout scene 6. In Act II, throughout scene 3. The traveller was also used to cover in-one scenes.

In the original production, Bernie and Cynthia's table was located in the audience, facing the D.L. corner of the stage.

Harry makes his first entrance in Act I scene 1 through the audience, and his exit in Act I scene 7 through the audience. Bernie makes his exit in Act I scene 7 through the audience.

SCENES AND MUSICAL NUMBERS

ACT I

1. Overture

SCENE 1—A SEMI-CHIC CABARET
2. "She Just Walked In" .... Harry and Ensemble
3. "A Man with a Problem" ...... Cynthia, Harry, Bernie

SCENE 2—INSIDE AND OUTSIDE A FINE BIG FACTORY
4. "Beautiful Day" .... The Company

SCENE 3—THE CABARET

SCENE 4—THROUGHOUT A HUGE METROPOLITAN HOSPITAL

SCENE 5—THE CABARET

SCENE 6—ALL OVER
5. "Commitment" .... The Company

SCENE 7—THE CABARET
6. "How Can I Tell?" .... Cynthia

ACT II

SCENE 1—DOWN IN THE VALLEY
7. "San Fernando" .... Harry, Bernie, Mr. Mann

SCENE 2—THE CABARET
8. "Give a Cheer" .... Bernie

SCENE 3—WITHIN THE SHADOW OF CHARITABLE INSTITUTIONS, INC.
9. "The Philanthropist's Progress"— A Cautionary Cantata,
    I. Aria .... Cynthia
    II. Recitative and Duet .... Harry, Cynthia
    III. Scene .... Mr. Mann, Harry
    IV. Grand Trio .... Cynthia, Harry, Mr. Mann
    V. Finaletto .... Mr. Mann, Cynthia
    VI. Arietta .... Harry
    VII. Scene and Finale .... Harry, Mr. Mann,
                             Bernie, Cynthia

SCENE 4—THE CABARET
10. "Who Wants to Work?" .... The Company

4

MONEY

PROLOGUE

Harry Clay enters through the audience during the overture. Mr.
Mann, as maitre d' beckons him to a table which Harry declines.
Mr. Mann points out several other tables, but none are good enough
for Harry. Finally, Harry decides to climb onto the stage. Mr.
Mann pantomimes "no!" Harry extracts a huge wad of money
from his pocket and hands a bill to Mr. Mann, then attempts to
get on stage again. Mr. Mann takes the money, pantomimes that
it's still impossible for Harry to use the stage. Harry gives him
another bill and Mr. Mann relents. Harry climbs onstage as the
overture ends. Cynthia and Bernie sit at a table D. L.

ACT I

SCENE 1

HARRY. Hiya. I'm incredibly wealthy. I am son and heir to the
oldest *nouveau-riche* family on the Eastern Seaboard. I was born
with a silver spoon, a New York town house and summers on the
Riviera in my mouth. Due to my extreme wealth, I have never
found it necessary to work for a living, so I have spent the greater
part of my life in a search for perfection. Perfection in the form
of a woman. I've looked everywhere in the world that first class
transportation could take me, alas, I've been unable to find the
one perfect woman. (*He sees Cynthia.*) That's her. (*Music under.
Sings.*)
   Excuse my grin, but look who just walked in,
   The girl who's gonna make my world begin to spin walked in,
   I'd have known her anywhere, and I swear I'm gonna get her,
   Though as yet I haven't met her, she just walked in.

I search for years, and then the girl appears,
And in a minute, wham! I'm in it,
Cue applause and cheers.
Wave flags and shoot off flares, light up the sky above me,
The girl who's gonna love me walked in.
(*Speaks.*) Waiter, flowers for this table. And a clean glass. (*Sings.*)
I'd have known you anywhere, and I swear I'm gonna get you.
(*Speaks.*) Waiter, bring the lady a fur coat. (*Sings.*)
My fondest hopes, my wildest dreams,
You make all of them real.
Wanna shout it to the world, tell everybody of it.
She just walked in.
(*Speaks.*) And now, for your dancing and listening pleasure . . .
(*He hands money to piano players. They sing a choral back-ground.*) A little more light on this table please. Surprise pink.
That's nice. Waiter—a chicken salad sandwich! (*Sings.*)
It's a miracle, I wax lyrical,
Let me hear a college cheer.
WAITER. Hip hoo-ray. Hip hoo-ray.
HARRY.
Excuse my grin, but look who just walked in,
The girl who's gonna make my world begin to spin walked in,
I'd have known her anywhere, and I swear I'm gonna get her,
Though as yet I haven't met her, she just walked in.
I search for years, and then the girl appears,
And in a minute, wham! I'm in it, cue applause and cheers,
Wave flags and shoot off flares, light up the sky above me,
(*Waiter enters with lit sparkler and small American flag, which he waves.*)
The girl who's gonna love me walked in.
(*Speaks.*) How do you like me so far?
CYNTHIA. I beg your pardon?
HARRY. Aren't I the guy you've been looking for all your life?
The one perfect man?
BERNIE. What are you fella, some sort of a nut? Forget it,
Cynthia, he's some sort of a nut. (*To audience.*) He's a nut . . .
(*Music.*)
HARRY. You see, all my life I've been looking for the one perfect
woman, and that's you.
CYNTHIA. Oh, come on.

6

HARRY. I never figured that it wouldn't be mutual. Don't you like me at all?

CYNTHIA. I think you're kind of cute. Thanks for the sandwich.

HARRY. Chicken salad is just the start. I love you. Will you marry me?

BERNIE. I told you he's a nut. Come on, Cynthia, let's get . . .

CYNTHIA. Just a moment, Bernie. You were saying . . . ?

HARRY. Will you marry me?

BERNIE. Now look, fella, you don't come in here and ask a strange woman to marry you like that.

CYNTHIA. Don't make a scene, Bernie.

BERNIE. I'm not making a scene, but he comes in here and sings songs and buys sandwiches, I never heard of it.

CYNTHIA. Just sit quietly, Bernie, and watch the show.

BERNIE. For this I pay a five-dollar minimum?

HARRY. Now—where was I?

CYNTHIA. Marry me. You were going to marry me.

HARRY. Oh that's right. Will you marry me?

CYNTHIA. No.

HARRY. Aw, c'mon.

CYNTHIA. No. I mean, I don't even love you.

HARRY. You could learn to love me. Easy. Have some money.

CYNTHIA. Oh no, I couldn't do that.

HARRY. No really, I've got lots.

CYNTHIA. Oh no.

HARRY. Go ahead. Take it.

CYNTHIA. Well thank you.

HARRY. Now do you love me?

CYNTHIA. (Pocketing money.) It's not that simple.

HARRY. It's not?

CYNTHIA. No, it's not. I know it's every young girl's dream that someday she'll meet a rich, handsome man in white shoes who'll ask her to marry him. But now that it's actually happening it's not just a question I can answer right off. It requires serious thought, expert advice. I'll call my mother.

HARRY. Telephone! (One appears. She thanks waiter. Harry tips him. Music fades and out.)

CYNTHIA. Operator, I want Yonkers 8-6844, and hurry. Hello, Mother? When did he call? Mother, for heaven's sake, he's old enough to be your father. I know he's a doctor, Mother . . . It's

7

not my last chance, Mother, please. Yes, that's what I called about Mother—I've met this very attractive affluent young man and he's made me an offer. Sure marriage, Momma, otherwise would I call you? What's his name? (*Whispers to Harry.*) What's your name?

HARRY. (*Whispers.*) Harry. Harry Clay.

CYNTHIA. (*Whispers.*) Hi. I'm Cynthia. Cynthia Burgess. That's my friend, Bernie Bartok.

HARRY. (*Whispers.*) Hi, Cynthia. Hello Bernie, how are ya?

BERNIE. (*Whispers.*) How do you do? What am I whispering for?

CYNTHIA. (*Into phone.*) Harry, Momma. His name is Harry Clay. Yeah, Bernie's here. They're talking. Anyway Momma, this handsome rich fellow wants to know will I marry him. She says yes. What does he do? He doesn't do anything, Momma, he is very comfortable. Loaded, yeah. What? No, he's not a doctor, I told you. Momma, it is possible to be rich and not be a doctor. Yes, I'll be home tonight. Mother, don't wait up. Mother, I hate chicken soup. Goodbye. (*Hangs up.*) Jewish mothers.

HARRY. Are you Jewish?

CYNTHIA. You don't have to be Jewish to have a Jewish mother.

HARRY. What did she say?

CYNTHIA. Who listens? Like always, she thinks I should marry a professional man.

HARRY. Why?

CYNTHIA. Because she wants to know he earns a nice living.

HARRY. I live nice.

CYNTHIA. But you don't earn it.

HARRY. But just sitting here I make more money than anybody who works. I don't have to work. I'm loaded.

CYNTHIA. You're not listening. You see Harry, Love is more than money. I should be able to help the man I love—start with him at the very bottom and share his joys and sorrows as he goes through life working with a goal in mind. With all your money you don't need me.

HARRY. Yes I do need you.

CYNTHIA. Then you're insecure.

HARRY. I'm perfectly secure.

CYNTHIA. I've seen the way you throw money around, buying sandwiches like there's no tomorrow. You call that secure? You must have had a miserable childhood.

HARRY. Cynthia, listen to me. I had a perfectly happy child-hood . . .

CYNTHIA. Harry, you can tell me.

HARRY. I am telling you. (*Music.*)

CYNTHIA. (*Sings.*)
I know, no don't tell me,
I know you've got problems,
Don't keep it so deep inside
It's better to open wide,
And say you're unhappy,
It's nothing that you ought to hide.

HARRY.
I'm not unhappy, I never have been
I've got no problems, just look at me grin

CYNTHIA.
You must have problems, at least one or two
Without a problem, what good could I be to a man like you?

HARRY. (*Spoken.*) In other words, Cynthia, you want me to be . . . ?

CYNTHIA. (*Sings.*)
A man with a problem, is a man I can love
A man to support and comfort is the sort I'm dreaming of.
When he is unhappy, I have carefully planned
To tenderly stroke his brow to show him how I understand.
If you have a problem
Then you're perfect for me
With all of your problems
Don't you see how really happy we could be?

HARRY. (*Spoken.*) Do you mean that if I have a problem you'll stay with me and help me work it out?

CYNTHIA. (*Spoken.*) It would certainly help.

HARRY. (*Spoken.*) In that case . . . I'm sure I can find some-thing . . . let me see . . . (*Sings.*)
No wait, no don't tell me
I've thought of a problem
Last Tuesday at half past two
The light in my bathroom blew

9

How's that for a problem?
Has that ever happened to you?

CYNTHIA.

That's not exactly
What I had in mind
But keep on trying
They're easy to find

HARRY.

Let's see, I'm thinking
I'm racking my brain

(*Snap.*)

I missed a taxi
And wouldn't you know it began to rain

CYNTHIA.

Now you see you're getting closer
Right down to the heart and core of it
Underneath that smile you're wretched
You'll agree as you think more of it
And I will help you solve your . . .

HARRY.

How about the time my folks sent me to camp without my
name tapes
How the other kids laughed.
And what about the day the downstairs butler quit
Leaving us upset and understaffed.

CYNTHIA.

Servant problems are the start of something seriously wrong
with . . .

HARRY.

And once I found a moth hole after I had put my suit on

CYNTHIA.

You're trying

HARRY.

And once while eating split pea soup I couldn't find a crouton

CYNTHIA.

Keep going

HARRY.

I remember something most upsetting in my past

CYNTHIA.

Oh I can hardly wait

HARRY.

Yes before a date my shoelace broke and I was kinda late.

CYNTHIA.

How you must have suffered.

HARRY.

Yeah I had to change my shoes and everything.

CYNTHIA. (*Spoken.*) There you see? You do have problems.

HARRY. (*Sings.*)

How marvellous. I have problems.

How wonderful I feel

You've made me the happiest guy in the world.

(*Speaks.*) Now that I've really found myself, will you stay with me and be by my side and share everything?

CYNTHIA. No. That's something you have to do for yourself.

HARRY. How?

CYNTHIA. Get a job. Then you'll *really* have problems.

HARRY. All right, Cynthia, I'll do it for you. I'll work and slave and get to the top. How do I get a job?

CYNTHIA. Easy. I know someone who works in an employment agency.

HARRY. I'll *go* there.

CYNTHIA. Oh Harry, you've found something money can't buy. Work!

HARRY. Thank heavens I discovered it in time. I'm going out there and meet my problems head on.

CYNTHIA. And I'll be behind you every step of the way.

HARRY. Oh no. By my side.

HARRY & CYNTHIA. (*Sing.*)

A man with a problem is a man with a dream

With both of us there to share it how divine that dream will
    seem

HARRY.	CYNTHIA.
With all of my problems	He's coming around
I am out of the dark	At last he's been found
I'm off to the chilly world	Ooooooooohhhhhh
To break my back and make my mark	
	He needs me
Thank God I'm unhappy	
With troubles galore	

11

Yes I'm gonna build a moun-
tain
Climb atop it, slide back
down   CYNTHIA.   BERNIE.
And climb some more   He needs me   He needs her
HARRY.
I'm gonna shoot for the sun
Grab for the moon
Outta my way, comin' there soon
Gotta make tracks, no time to pause
I've got it made, and all because . . .
I'm unhappy
CYNTHIA.
He's unhappy.
BERNIE.
Son of a bitch.

(*Music continues on applause. Exit Harry and Cynthia. Music fade and out as Bernie speaks.*)

ACT I

SCENE 2

BERNIE. (*At his table.*) See? She's forgotten all about me. It's not the first time, but it's gonna be the last. I'll show her. (*Crosses to stage.*) I'll build my own mountain. I'll go to an employment agency too! I'll quit my job and go to an employment agency. I'll climb and claw and struggle my way to the top. I'm gonna be rich, just like he is. Look out world, here comes Bernie Bartok. (*Alarm bell rings.*) Gosh. (*Glances at watch.*) It's nine o'clock tomorrow morning. I'll be late for my job interview. (*Music.*) Look at the fine big factory the employment agency has sent me to. I guess they know their business all right. I'm anxious to learn the results of the psychological placement test I took to determine what sort of job I'm suited for.

MAN. (*He has clipboard and pencil.*) Mr. Bartok, will you come in please?

BERNIE. (*To audience.*) Excuse me.

MAN. Now Mr. Bartok, I have here your psychological preference test in which you were given a choice of three things, asked to select one of them and stick a pin hole through it.

BERNIE. Yes sir.

MAN. I notice here you were given three choices: would you rather build a birdhouse, read a book or bake a cake. And you selected build a birdhouse. Mr. Bartok, this is 1964. People don't build birdhouses anymore. You can just go into any store and buy one, you see what I mean?

BERNIE. Yes sir, but I think I can explain that. You see, I made the wrong choice. What I meant to select was "read a book."

MAN. Oh yeah? What kind of a book?

BERNIE. What was the third choice?

MAN. Bake a cake.

BERNIE. That's what I'd rather do.

MAN. I thought so, you faggot. Out. (*Music.*)

HARRY. (*Enters.*) Well, look at the fine big factory the employment agency has sent me to. I guess they know their business all right. I'm anxious to . . .

MAN. Mr. Clay, will you come in, please?

HARRY. (*To audience.*) Excuse me. (*Passes by Bernie.*) Hi, Benny.

BERNIE. Bernie!

MAN. I've been looking over your placement test, and I notice on the question "Would you rather build a birdhouse, read a book or bake a cake" you have listed all three.

HARRY. Yes sir.

MAN. As a matter of fact, you've marked every selection on the entire test.

HARRY. Yes sir. I believe an idle brain is the devil's plaything.

MAN. Well spoken, Clay. We can use go-getters of your stripe in this company.

HARRY. Oh thank you, sir. When do I start?

MAN. Whoa. Hold on there a minute, young fellow. First we have to determine what sort of job you're equipped to do. Tell me a little about your experience.

HARRY. What experience?

MAN. What sort of work have you done?

HARRY. I've never worked.

MAN. At all?

HARRY. Never. That's my problem. I just sit around all day doing nothing and making a whole lot of money.

MAN. Well those are rather peculiar qualifications for employment. As a matter of fact, the only job around here for someone who sits around all day doing nothing and making a whole lot of money is Chairman of the Board.

HARRY. Chairman of the Board?

MAN. Yes. Come to think of it, we have an opening. Are you interested?

HARRY. Interested? (*Music.*) But wait . . . what would Cynthia say? She'd say . . . (*Cynthia's head appears through curtain.*)

CYNTHIA. Chairman of the Board? What would that prove? You'd just sit around all day doing nothing and making a whole lot of money. (*Music out.*)

HARRY. That's what she'd say.

CYNTHIA. No I wouldn't.

HARRY. Yes, you would. (*Cynthia's head disappears.*) No! I cannot accept. She wants me to work, and work I must. Do you have an opening for a worker?

MAN. Well, for a man of no training, experience or proven ability, about the only thing we have other than Chairman of the Board is the mailroom.

HARRY. I'll take it. I'll become a mailman.

MAN. I don't think you quite . . .

HARRY. Oh thank you sir. When do I start?

MAN. Tomorrow morning at nine. And good luck.

HARRY. Thank you sir. (*Harry exits.*)

MAN. What a shame. He'd have made a wonderful Chairman of the Board. (*Blackout. Music. Lights up on Cynthia and Bernie waiting for Harry.*)

HARRY. (*Entering.*) Cynthia, I made it. I start in the mailroom tomorrow.

CYNTHIA. The mailroom?

HARRY. Yeah. Isn't it wonderful.

CYNTHIA. Oh Harry, I'm so happy for you.

HARRY. Me too. (*Music out.*)

MAN. (*Entering.*) Strike.

HARRY. What?

MAN. We're on strike. Don't just stand there. Picket.

HARRY. But I haven't started work yet.

14

MAN. You call yourself a worker, you're on strike.

CYNTHIA. Well then, by George, he's on strike.

MAN. Good man. (*Music under.*)

BERNIE. Here's my chance to get the better of him. I'll become a company scab.

HARRY. I don't know what to think. No sooner do I find employment than I and my fellow workers are called out on strike.

CYNTHIA. Don't worry, Harry. I'll be beside you.

HARRY. No no, this is a picket line, remember? Be behind me.

MAN. (*Sings.*)
Men of the working classes,
Rise to the day with a shout.
Get up off your downtrodden masses
And walk right out.

ALL.
When there's a girl right behind you
When she is a girl whom you like,
The birds sing a song to remind you
It's a beautiful day for a strike.

On a calm silver lake couples rowing
Or off on a picnic or hike.
A fresh water breeze gently blowing,
It's a beautiful day for a strike.

CYNTHIA. (*Bernie appears with picket signs, hands one to man, one to Harry and keeps one. All signs read "strike."*)
When the world is in blossom
Spring is my cup of tea.
So my love don't play possum,
Every thrush in the thicket is singing "go picket"
So picket with me.

ALL.
Picket with me!
On warm summer nights we will creep out

CYNTHIA.
And ride on our built for two bike.
But now there are finks we must keep out.

15

ALL.
   It's a beautiful day, what a glorious day,
   It's a beautiful day for a strike.
(*Man turns sign around. It reads: "Down with Management." Harry turns his around. It reads "Up with Labor." Bernie turns his sign around. It reads "And Vice Versa."*)
   See the buds as they glitter
   On that old maple tree
   Hear the birdies a-twitter
   Every sparrow and hawk out
   Is singing let's walk out
   So walk out with me
CYNTHIA.
   Unfair!
ALL.
   On a hammock when everything's quiet
   You'll swing with your Molly or Mike,
CYNTHIA.
   But pardon us now while we riot! And I mean riot!
ALL.
   It's a beautiful day, what a glorious day,
   It's a beautiful day for a strike!
(*End of song.*)
MAN. Hooray, the strike is over. We've won the day.
ALL. Hooray! (*Musical sting.*)
MAN. Management has acceded to our every demand.
ALL. Hooray! (*Musical sting.*)
HARRY. We've won. We've won. What have we won?
MAN. (* = *musical stings.*) All our demands. Triple inverted over-undertime,* our previous salary squared,* pensions for friends,* the no-hour week,* retirement after two years,* no automation without representation.* In other words . . .
HARRY. We'll be able to sit around all day doing nothing and making a whole lot of money.
BERNIE & MAN. (*Sing.*)
   It's a beautiful day for a strike!
(*Blackout. Music. Music fade and out as lights up and Cynthia speaks.*)

16

Up on Cynthia in front of curtain. She has the phone. It rings.

CYNTHIA. Hello? Oh hello, Momma. Yes, Harry was launched in a business career, but he quit. No, Momma, he wasn't fired, he quit.

HARRY. (*Entering.*) I had no choice. I was no better off there than I was before.

CYNTHIA. What, Momma? Well, he wasn't doing anything before and that's what he'd have been doing if he was working. Oh well, Momma, let's face it—you won't approve of *anybody* unless he's a doctor. (*Musical sting. Lightbulb.*)

HARRY. A doctor! Why not? It only takes eight years.

CYNTHIA. Momma, do we have to go through this with every man I meet?

HARRY. (*To himself.*) I mean a doctor is interested in more than money—he's interested in healing.

CYNTHIA. (*Into phone.*) Absolutely not.

HARRY. (*To himself.*) Yes!

CYNTHIA. (*Into phone.*) No! For heaven's sake, Mother, I can't ask him to go and start medical school.

HARRY. I'll see you, Cynthia.

CYNTHIA. Where are you going?

HARRY. I'm going to medical school. Want to walk me?

CYNTHIA. I have to hang up now, Momma, I'm walking Harry to medical school. I'm here, don't scream. Just calm down and I'll put him on. (*To Harry.*) Momma wants to talk to you.

HARRY. Hello, Mrs. Burgess. I don't know what I'm going to specialize in—I haven't even applied to medical school yet. Look— you don't have to call me "doctor." Just call me Harry, Mrs. Burgess. To me it's what? Oh, thank you, Mrs. Buxbaum. Just a minute—here's Cynthia. (*To Cynthia.*) She approves!

CYNTHIA. That's news? (*To phone.*) Yes Momma. I may not be home eight years from tonight. Goodbye. (*Music under.*) Oh Harry . . .

HARRY. Yes?

CYNTHIA. Oh Harry, I'll . . . I'll . . . I'll walk you.

HARRY. Wait—I don't even know the way.

CYNTHIA. I know the way. (*They exit as music swells. Fade music as Bernie speaks.*)

BERNIE. (*At his table.*) There they go again. She came in here with me, remember? Well I remember. She came in with me. And now she's walking him to medical school. Speaking candidly, I would venture to say that this is very possibly the worst day I've had all week. (*Lights dim.*) No, the second to worst . . . (*Lights dim further. Music under.*) No . . . (*Dimout.*)

ACT I

SCENE 4

In the darkness, we hear a Voice, amplified on mike.

VOICE. Once again we present "Young Intern Clay," a story dedicated to the selfless men and women who, in the courageous service of the medical profession, work their ass off in our nation's hospitals. (*Lights. Cynthia is in Nurse's cap. Man enters. Fade music as Cynthia speaks.*)

CYNTHIA. Difficult operation, doctor?

MAN. Very. Ruptured appendix. Had a devil of a time getting it back together. (*Harry enters.*)

HARRY. (*To Cynthia.*) Hiya. (*To Man.*) Here's that blood count you ordered, doctor.

MAN. Never mind about that, Clay. I've diagnosed Mrs. O'Leary. I'm afraid it's a post-prandial obstruction.

HARRY. No!

MAN. Au contraire—yes! We'll have to go in there and perform a Schleswig-Holstein. The operation will be unsuccessful, of course.

HARRY. It will?

MAN. It always is. Clay, you've got to go in there and tell that old woman she's going to die.

HARRY. Why me?

MAN. Why you? My boy, I'd like to tell you a little story. (*Music under.*) I remember a rocking horse . . . a beautiful dappled rocking horse with a white mane and golden bridle. And I remember a little boy, his nose pressed against the toy store window, who

18

wanted that rocking horse more than he wanted anything in the whole world. He dreamed of that rocking horse. He dreamed of riding it out of the shabby world which surrounded him. And then came that little boy's birthday. How he hoped and prayed for that beautiful rocking horse. He did not get that rocking horse, Clay.

HARRY. He didn't?

MAN. He did not. But out of that disappointment came knowledge. And as you may have guessed, Clay, that little boy was you.

HARRY. He was? (*Music out.*)

MAN. Yes. So you go in there and tell that old woman she's going to die.

HARRY. Yes sir. (*He goes off.*)

VOICE. Dr. Daniels, wanted in obstetrics.

CYNTHIA. That reminds me, doctor, there's a riot in the maternity ward.

MAN. I'm not surprised.

CYNTHIA. And post-operative complications on the Landers case.

MAN. I don't want to hear about it.

VOICE. Dr. Moriarty, wanted in 13 states. (*Man and Cynthia nod knowingly.*)

HARRY. (*Entering.*) I . . . I told Mrs. O'Leary, doctor.

MAN. Oh yeah? How'd she take it?

HARRY. She hit me right in the mouth.

MAN. Common reaction. Well, it will soon be all over.

HARRY. How long does she have, doctor?

MAN. Who knows? She may live to be a hundred. She's healthy as a horse. I did it for you, my boy. Next time you'll find it a little easier.

HARRY. Gee, Doctor Mann, you're a good wise man.

MAN. Well, maybe you'll find I'm not really the gruff old bear I may seem to be. (*He passes Cynthia and growls.*) By the way, how are things coming between you and Nurse Burgess?

HARRY. Gosh, doctor . . .

MAN. Now now—I may be an old gaffer, but I can still tell when a girl has set her cap for someone.

HARRY. We're both pretty busy and . . .

MAN. Oh you don't have to tell me! (*Music under.*) It wasn't so many years ago that I was an intern at this very hospital—and I have my memories. Just remember one thing, Clay. I don't think I have to tell you that these girls work as long and as hard as we do. For maybe sixteen, seventeen hours at a time they have to live in a world of suffering, where they must forget that they're women. Working around men all day, never allowed to show their feelings, never allowed to express emotion of any kind. Naturally when they get off work, (*Music fade and out.*) well, they sometimes— just be careful. Some of them have incredible diseases.

CYNTHIA. The patient is ready for surgery, doctor.

MAN. Thank you, nurse. Nurse Burgess is assisting us in the operation. Notice the way she looked at you? Horny as a toad. Well, back to the old abbatoir. (*Music under throughout remainder of scene. Throughout the following, constant pantomime of the preparation and procedure of an operation.*) How are the studies progressing, Clay?

HARRY. Just fine, sir. Most interesting pituitary yesterday. Terribly acute condition.

MAN. How so?

HARRY. Well, I'm not so hot on medical terminology. It was just sort of screwed up.

MAN. Hmmm. Clay, medical terms are one thing you'll have to learn. Can't win the patient's confidence if you tell them their pituitary is screwed up. Try something like "glaucoma" for real shock effect.

HARRY. Doesn't that have something to do with the eyes?

MAN. Oh? Scalpel. (*Musical sting.*) Well Clay, what have you been picking up in the wards?

HARRY. Well, I've been learning a great deal about patient psychology, handling people, and that sort of thing.

MAN. We'll have to get you out in the field, Clay. There's a lot more to doctoring than what you've learned. For example, what do you know about double parking?

HARRY. You mean on house calls?

MAN. Who makes house calls?

CYNTHIA. More oxygen, doctor?

MAN. No thanks, I'm driving. Now about fee splitting. Scissors.

HARRY. I know what that is. Sending a patient to a specialist and splitting a much higher fee. I couldn't do something like that.

MAN. And why, if I may be so bold, not?

HARRY. I couldn't overcharge people who are sick and can't afford to pay.

MAN. Poor people? Forget about them. They come in here and

never pay off anyway. The rich, my boy. Take a lesson from Robin Hood—bleed those bastards. Ooops—coagulant. (*Nurse pantomimes handing him a shaker which he shakes into patient, then over his left shoulder.*) Now here are some interesting methods of fee splitting you might not know about: kickbacks from pharmacies, recommending a particular brand of aspirin, diet foods, some of those companies will pay through the nose . . .

HARRY. I don't like it. I'd just as soon wash my hands of the whole thing.

MAN. You should have washed your hands before you came in here. As a matter of fact, we both should have. Sponge.

CYNTHIA. Sponge.

MAN. Oh hello there. Look Clay, understand something. We're doctors. Healers. Easers of pain. We've got a good public image. Now we've earned that image and we shouldn't be ashamed to take advantage of it. Clamp.

HARRY. That sounds pretty hypocritical to me.

MAN. Well, we all take the hypocritic oath. Clamp!

HARRY. Cratic.

MAN. No, clamp.

CYNTHIA. No more clamps.

MAN. Okay, make it a sponge. We're businessmen, Clay. We have something to sell here. A product. That product is health. We package it, advertise it, and push it over the counter. (*He almost pushes patient over while gesturing.*) Oooops, sorry. Scalpel.

HARRY. That's terrible. If I have a talent for medicine, if that's something I can do for people, then I'll do it. I ask nothing for myself.

MAN. Now hold on a minute, boy. Listen. (*He carelessly jabs scalpel into patient.*) Medical men are people. We're human. It's true that some of us are healer-dealers. It's true that some of us forget our calling in the pursuit of the almighty dollar. Some of us think more of having the right address than of our duties. There are some among us who will refuse to make house calls, overcharge patients, split fees . . . some of us do that. But only a very, very small majority. Remember that.

HARRY. I will, Doctor Mann, I will.

MAN. Clay, I see now that you have the true spirit of a doctor of medicine. I'm sorry I had to sound the way I did, but I think you've learned from it.

21

HARRY. Oh I have, Dr. Mann, I have. Thank you. I feel much better now.

MAN. You do.

HARRY. Oh yes, sir.

MAN. Good. That'll be twenty dollars for therapy.

HARRY. Twenty dollars!?

MAN. You feel better, you pay for it. If you think I give this stuff away, you're a damn fool—and that's another twenty dollars for diagnosis. Now sew this guy up and be in my office in ten minutes with the cash, check, or money order. (*Exits.*)

HARRY. I've done it again. I've failed. I'll never make a good doctor. I don't need the money enough. I'm quitting. Nurse.

CYNTHIA. Yes, doctor?

HARRY. Sew this man up. (*Exits.*)

CYNTHIA. Yes, doctor. (*Looks at watch.*) Hey! It's five o'clock. Orderly!

BERNIE. Yes, nurse.

CYNTHIA. Sew this man up. (*Exits.*)

BERNIE. (*At table, wearing intern's cap.*) Yes, nurse. (*He goes to patient.*) Okay buddy, wake up. Hey buddy! You awake? Good. Now you take this needle and thread . . . (*Blackout. Music continues.*)

ACT I

SCENE 5

Lights up on Harry and Cynthia in front of the curtain. Music continues softly under dialogue.

HARRY. Well, that does it with me and the Medical Profession.

CYNTHIA. Momma will be so disappointed—she's already bought you a shingle.

HARRY. Sorry.

CYNTHIA. Well—maybe it *could* read: "Doctor Harry Clay— Attorney."

HARRY. No. No doctor, no lawyer—if I have to work, I want to work at something I believe in.

22

CYNTHIA. Harry, you're an idealist!

HARRY. Yeah? What do I believe in?

CYNTHIA. That's your trouble; you lack an ideal.

HARRY. As simple as that?

CYNTHIA. Certainly! Yes, certainly. You're the kind of a man who needs a cause he can fight for—you need to be committed to something. That's it—what you need is *commitment!*

HARRY. Commitment?

CYNTHIA. Of course!

HARRY. (*Sings.*)
Commitment, commitment
That's what I need, a commitment

CYNTHIA.
Commitment, commitment,
No doubt about it, right now he must have a commitment

HARRY.
But what?
What do I do, where do I go
How will I know when I've found it that it's a commitment?

ALL.
What do you care
Dig up a cause
If you can stand it
Stand up and demand it be followed
And that's a commitment

HARRY.
That's a commitment?—Gee!
I remember my dad, when he'd finally made his dough and
    retired
He got completely fired up about injustice in the world
And joined a committee . . .

ALL.
He joined a committee?

HARRY.
Yes, he joined the committee to deport Owen Lattimore
And free the Scottsboro boys
Now would you call that commitment?

ALL.

Yes. That's a commitment!

Like your dad—discover its joys!

HARRY.

Yes. I'll go out and be committed

Discover a noble cause, the way my dad found his

He didn't hold back, he went out and did it

Now I'm gonna fight, I'll fight for the right

Whatever it is

ALL.

Oh go out and be committed

Discover a noble cause that calls to you and then

You mustn't hold back, you must be committed

So take up the fight, and fight for the right

Forever amen.

(*Blackout.*)

ACT I

Scene 6

Throughout this scene, Mr. Mann appears as various characters. His head only is seen through different slots in the curtain. The same applies to Bernie for his one appearance. Music is continuous throughout, with cues as indicated in vocal score.

HARRY. Is this the Veteran's Legion of America?

MAN. What?

HARRY. Is this the Veteran's Legion of America?

MAN. That's right. You a member?

HARRY. No.

MAN. Get out.

HARRY. No, you see, I'm thinking of becoming a member.

MAN. Oh that's differently. You a veteran?

HARRY. No.

MAN. So what?

HARRY. You see, I heard about your excellent patriotic achievements, and since I'm searching for commitment, this seemed like the ideal place. You know, Americanism and everything.

MAN. Could you run a movie projector?

HARRY. Movie projector?

MAN. For the dirty movies. Every Thursday, after the pledge-allegiance, we show dirty movies.

HARRY. That's not Americanism.

MAN. Listen kid, we show these movies, lots of Americans come to watch 'em.

HARRY. But . . .

MAN. I tell you kid, sometimes this here place is Mexico City, USA. Interested? Three hundred bucks a year, that includes the picnic.

HARRY. You don't understand.

MAN. It also includes funny convention hats, a long black cigar and a squirting poppy.

HARRY. Wait a minute.

MAN. Wait'll you attend one of our conventions. Talk about drunk—and broads.

HARRY. That's not what I want at all. I want something patriotic and worthwhile. But thank you. (*Exits.*)

MAN. We get lots of guys like him in here. No wonder we're so far behind the Russians.

CYNTHIA & BERNIE. (*Sing.*)
Commitment, commitment,
How did you like your commitment?

HARRY. (*Sings.*)
I was amazed, I was appalled
Who knows what it meant
It wasn't my kind of commitment.

CYNTHIA. (*Sings.*)
Though it may hurt, try it again,
Nose to the grindstone and ear to the ground
And before long you've found a commitment—like this!

HARRY. Is this the American Minutemen to Preserve America from Everyone Else Every Minute?

MAN. Yes.

HARRY. I seek commitment to a patriotic organization.

MAN. Look no further. That's an order.

HARRY. Wait a minute. How does your organization function?

25

MAN. We keep a weather eye peeled for enemies of democracy.
(*He stares intently at Harry.*)
HARRY. Have you found any?
MAN. You better believe it.
HARRY. What do you do with these people once you've found them?
MAN. We get 'em. Ever hear of Thurgood Frong?
HARRY. Never.
MAN. That's 'cause we got 'em. We're after the big fish now. He's pretended to be a friend of the west, but we're on to him and his peaceful co-existence. We're on to him, we're zeroing in on him, and we're gonna get him.
HARRY. Khrushchev!
MAN. Who?
BERNIE. (*Sings.*)
　How did you like your commitment?
HARRY.
　Who do I ask, what do I do?
　Where do I look, in the telephone book, for commitment?
CYNTHIA.
　Don't ask a soul, find it yourself,
　Look very hard and in your own back yard
　You are likely to find a commitment.
HARRY. (*Spoken.*) Well, if you can't beat 'em, join 'em. Is this the Red Hammer and Sickle Socialist Labor Workers People's Peace Party Group?
MAN. (*Now wearing eyeglasses.*) Yes it is.
HARRY. Just exactly how does your organization function?
MAN. Oh you know. We stir up trouble—demonstrate in front of the UN, picket, make speeches in Union Square, blow up stuff, things like that.
HARRY. In other words . . .
MAN. Right. We're an FBI front group.
BERNIE. (*Sings.*)
　Oh go out and be committed . . .
BERNIE & CYNTHIA.
　So take up the fight
　And fight for the right
BERNIE, CYNTHIA & HARRY.
　Forever, amen.

HARRY. Is this the National Council for Everybody in the World Being Equal to Each Other?

MAN. Right you are.

HARRY. What exactly are your aims?

MAN. We believe in the freedom of all peoples, regardless of race or religious belief, in freedom to worship as one chooses, and that equality is the only road to a happier world.

HARRY. That's exactly what I'm interested in. Is there any way I can help you to further these aims?

MAN. Sure . . . here's the gimmick.

CYNTHIA & BERNIE.
   Discover a noble cause that calls to you and then . . .

HARRY. Is this the organization of American Grey Haired Mothers to Preserve Our Basic Ideals?

MAN. That's right sonny.

HARRY. Just exactly what do you do?

MAN. We're a hate group.

BERNIE & CYNTHIA.
   Commitment, commitment,
   You can't find a commitment.

HARRY. Is this the United Nudists of America?

MAN. Yes. Excuse me for not getting up.

HARRY. I'm looking for a commitment and I'd like to learn a little more about your organization. Why are you so dedicated to nudism?

MAN. Oh, you can't see boobies through a parka.

BERNIE & CYNTHIA.
   Commitment, commitment . . .

HARRY. Is this the Republican National Committee?

MAN. Right.

HARRY. What do you do?

MAN. What can we do?

BERNIE & CYNTHIA.
   Commitment, commitment . . .

HARRY. Is this the National Conference of Christians and Jews?

MAN. Yes . . .

BERNIE. (*Head thru curtain.*) And no.

BERNIE & CYNTHIA.
   Commitment, commitment.

27

HARRY. Is this the . . . (Sees man wearing Mickey Mouse ears.)
. . . forget it.
BERNIE & CYNTHIA.
   Commitment, commitment.
HARRY. Are you Billy Graham?
BERNIE. No, I'm not. (Squirts Harry in the face with a water pistol.)
HARRY. Is this the Foundation for Brotherly Love?
MAN. Yes. I love you. (Blackout.)
ALL. (In darkness, singing.)
   Once we're all committed, we'll be fine.
(Music out.)

ACT I

Scene 7

HARRY. That's it, Cynthia.
CYNTHIA. Oh Harry, you've found an organization!
HARRY. That's right.
CYNTHIA. I'm so excited for you. Which one is it?
HARRY. National Airline Passengers Association.
CYNTHIA. I've never heard of them. What do they do?
HARRY. They get on airplanes and they get out of town. Goodbye, Cynthia.
CYNTHIA. Harry, come back here. What are you saying?
HARRY. I've had it. This is all too much for me. I've got to get away from here and sort things out.
CYNTHIA. Oh Harry, for a minute I thought you had failed, but you're trying again, aren't you?
HARRY. I am?
CYNTHIA. Yes. You're off to seek the simple life, the quiet contemplative existence. Maybe you can write a book—like Thoreau.
HARRY. No! I don't want to write a book. I don't want to do anything. I just want to get away from here.
CYNTHIA. Yes yes, Harry. And I'll be beside you.
HARRY. No! You'll be behind me—as far behind me as you can get. Like right here. I want to get away to the fresh clean air,

where there are no people around to louse things up. Goodbye, Cynthia. I'm leaving you.

CYNTHIA. Harry! Aren't you ever coming back?

HARRY. Of course I'm coming back. (*Exits.*) Geez!

CYNTHIA. So long, Harry, have a nice time. Send a postcard! (*Goes to table.*) I've driven him away. (*Cries loudly.*)

BERNIE. I couldn't help overhearing your sobs.

CYNTHIA. Oh Bernie. What's the matter with me?

BERNIE. You cry too loud.

CYNTHIA. What am I going to do?

BERNIE. Now look, Cynthia. Even though you've treated me like dirt, I don't mind. I'll take care of you and it will be just like it was before you met . . . him. You'll see. I admit I'm not very rich or even very handsome, but I'm a good worker and I'll do my best to provide for you.

CYNTHIA. Oh Bernie. I'm so unhappy. (*Sobs.*) Why do I keep after him like that, making him do things he doesn't want to do, driving him away from me? Why can't I be satisfied with him the way he is?

BERNIE. I don't know, Cynthia. Maybe you're just a pushy broad.

CYNTHIA. I think maybe you're right, Bernie. Now will you do something for me?

BERNIE. Anything.

CYNTHIA. Get run over.

BERNIE. But Cynthia . . .

CYNTHIA. Come on, Bernie—out in the street—under a car . . .

BERNIE. Cynthia!

CYNTHIA. Bernie . . .

BERNIE. I know. Under a car. (*He exits.*)

CYNTHIA. He's right. I'm a pushy broad. (*Music under. Telephone rings. Waiter brings Cynthia the phone. She answers.*) Hello? Oh Momma, shut up! (*She sings.*)

    I know, no don't tell me
    I know I'm uncertain
    It isn't that I'm aloof
    It's just that I need some proof
    I know I'm uncertain
    But what other way can I be?

    How can I tell, can I tell right away,

29

Can I stand here and say look no more, this is he
How can I tell, where's a sign I can see,
Am I fooling my heart, is my heart fooling me
Though I'll gladly confess when he catches my eye
What a fourth of July that can be
How can I tell if the man of my dreams
Is the right sort of person for me.

A man with a mission
My conscience suggests
A man with an office
My mother requests
A man who will need me
That's Redbook's advice
A man who attracts me
Might also be nice.

How can I tell, can I tell from a glance
Should I make an advance or forget it and flee
Is there no way to tell if the man of my dreams
Is the right sort of man
Right sort of type
Right sort of person for me.
How can I tell . . .
How can I tell . . .
Can I tell.

(*Music fade and out.*)

MAN. (*As waiter, fighting back tears.*) There will now be a brief
intermission for open discussion and the consumption of beverages.
(*Music.*)

END OF ACT I

ACT II

SCENE 1

Entr'acte

Cynthia enters as "How Can I Tell" is played. Music fade and out.

CYNTHIA. When we left our hero . . . when our hero left us . . . left me . . . he was headed out West to get away from it all and seek the simple life . . . And I love him for that . . . I love you, Harry Clay . . . (*Curtain opens revealing Harry in western garb.*) wherever you are . . . (*Music.*)

HARRY. (*Sings.*)

Livin's easy in my simple little lean to
In the San Fernando valley
Where the cactus smells like clover
And a fella sorta seems to feel at ease
In my easy livin' lean to in the splendor
Of the San Fernando valley
You can lie back with your boots off
Stick a straw between your teeth and shoot the breeze.

(*Speaks. Music under.*) Boy. This is really the life. All right. No pressures . . . no distractions. Time to sit back and concentrate on the important things . . . like life . . . and nature . . . and . . . rocks. Rocks! Boy. There's something we sure take for granted. But you try sitting there, not doing anything, just contemplating a rock. I'm telling you, it frees the mind. Don't laugh. You stare at a rock for a couple of hours with absolutely nothing to distract you and you'd be surprised at the images your mind conjures up—images such as wild parties . . . big parades . . . crowded streets . . . combined glee clubs . . . It certainly is a relief. Having no one around, I mean. To distract you. Or talk to you. Or anything . . . It's enough to make you want to sit right down and look at a rock . . . Aw—I've looked at *that* rock before—There

31

must be another rock around here someplace . . . Wait!—What's this I see?—Is it a mirage? No! It's another human being!—And he's coming this way! (*He primps madly.*) How do I look? (*Man enters menacingly, followed by Bernie. They both wear cowboy hats. Music out.*)

MAN. Howdy, stranger. (*Harry is practically climbing all over them.*)

HARRY. Hi! Howdy! Welcome! Pull up a rock—I'm Harry Clay. What did you say your name was? (*Musical sting.*)

MAN. I didn't. (*Musical sting.*)

BERNIE. If it's anything to you, he's Big Man around these parts.

MAN. This here's my side-kick, Black Bartok. (*Musical sting.*)

HARRY. Any relation to the composer?

MAN. Look—we didn't come here to shoot the breeze; we ain't got time for jawin'. We were sort of wonderin' what your idea was in settlin' down out here. We're simple folk. We lead a simple life, close to the soil, and we don't want . . .

BERNIE. We don't want no city fellers comin' out here with their fancified Eastern ways tryin' to change things.

MAN. Can it, Bartok. (*To Harry.*) We was just wonderin' what yer aimin' to do with this here spread.

HARRY. Well, you don't have to worry about me changing anything. That's what I came out here for. To find simple reality; I'm not going to change anything about this place.

MAN. (*Aghast.*) You're not going to change anything? You mean you're going to leave this miserable, rotten, rundown piece of property the way it is?

HARRY. Well, I might put in a little rock garden.

MAN. Well, let me tell you—I happen to represent a little committee, calls themselves the Welcome Wagon Vigilantes (*Musical sting.*) dedicated to keeping property values up and undesirable elements out. And we're not going to let you get away with this.

HARRY. I don't mean to cause no trouble.

MAN. And we don't mean to give you a hard time. We can be right neighborly, once we're sure you fit in.

HARRY. Fit in to what?

MAN. Fit in to the overall architectural pattern which the urban re-development league has planned for this neck of the woods. Now, I happen to represent a little organization calls themselves the OK Bar Lazy H Construction Company, and we would be proud to rustle you up a little split level ranch type bungalow.

HARRY. All I need is a simple shack.

MAN. Now hold on there pardner—stop—whoa! You're talkin' simple shack—when the style hereabouts runs to split level ranch-type bungalows . . .

BERNIE. . . . And they ain't room enough in this here town for the both of them.

HARRY. Why don't you just tell me what's expected of me around here.

MAN. Good, I think we're climbing into the saddle from the same side of the horse.

BERNIE. God, I wish I'd said *that*.

MAN. Why don't you just leave everything to us? I'm sure we can help you whip up a little homestead that'll fit right in with everything else around here. Of course, you'll be hankerin' for a decorator . . .

HARRY. A decorator?

MAN. It just so happens that I represent the gol-durndest little ol' interior decorator west of Dodge City.

HARRY. Who's that?

MAN. Black Bartok. (*Musical sting. Bernie walks slowly over to Harry and sticks out his hand.*)

BERNIE. Howdy, sweetie. (*Surveying the scene. Music under.*) I see something in a yummy sort of non-specific Spanish . . .

HARRY. I wanted something simple.

MAN. We're *makin'* it simple for you, friend.

BERNIE. . . . Over here would be a heavenly place for the conversation area, I reckon . . .

HARRY. Conversation area?

BERNIE. You know, precious, the chatterpit.

MAN. Now I happen to represent . . .

BERNIE. A free form arroyo, Swedish modern corral, an outrageous bunkhouse! Of course, I don't know what I'm going to do with all this ghastly cactus.

MAN. Can it, Bartok.

BERNIE. Canned cactus, what a mad idea! And over here—the gazebo.

HARRY. Please, keep it simple.

BERNIE. Simple? Buckaroos, it's going to be *basic!*

33

MAN. Buckaroos?

BERNIE. Oh I love it to death! It's going to be so *western!*

HARRY. (*Sings, with sarcastic indignation.*)
"Go west, young man" said what's his name
And he was right as rain
For that's the only place where simple values still remain—

BERNIE. (*Spoken.*) —And one of those marvellous horse things over the door!

HARRY. (*Sings.*)
Where simple, honest people still pursue their simple chores
In a simple outdoor setting that's as big as all outdoors.
So come with me, my lady, to a place where time stands still
Where you never take a taxi and you never take a pill.

HARRY, MAN & BERNIE. (*During song, Harry attempts to sneak away, but is drawn back by the others.*)

Livin's easy in my little hacienda in the San Fernando valley
You can sit on the veranda sniffin' zephyrs from the navel
orange trees
In my little hacienda midst the splendor of the San Fernando
valley
You can lie back with your boots off, stick a straw between
your teeth
And shoot the breeze

You'll appreciate the architect's attempt to capture early Cali-
fornia
Everything is done in subtle non-specific Spanish stucco topped
with tile
In the patio the muzak plays "Juanita" and I guess I'd better
warn ya:
Why that swimmin' pool that's shaped like Sutter's Mill
Just seems to whisper "stay awhile"

Stay awhile, stay awhile
Tie your troubles to a hitchin' post and smile
Rest a spell, rest a spell
If the world goes by without you—what the hell

Western atmosphere's enhanced by caref'lly landscaped man-
   made mesas in the distance
You'll especially like the mesquite scented sign in front which
   spells out "Shangri-Lodge"
From the moment you arrive, the spell of San Fernando
   crumbles all resistance
When John Wayne produced "The Alamo" he shot the final
   scene from my garage.

The chuck wagon in the kitchen is authentic and completely
   automatic
And the library is lined with rawhide covered first editions of
   Zane Grey
Jacob Epstein on commission did the bust of General Custer
   in the attic
In the bar the swingin' doors are softly singin' "welcome
   stranger, come and stay"

Come and stay, come and stay
Where the skies are never threatening or gray
Steal away, steal away
In the summer we have cook-outs every day.

Why not ride out to my forty acre hide-out in the San Fer-
   nando valley
Where Mount Baldy, slyly smiling, tips his snowy cap and
   looks the other way
To a rendezvous that's only known to you and me and maybe
   Rand McNally
In my San Fernando valley hacienda we can spend an endless
   day
Endless day, endless day
Steal away, steal away
Come and stay, come and stay
Steal away
Hmmmmmmmmmmmmmmmmmmmmmm
(*Harry steals away. Dimout. Music up. Fade and out as Cynthia
speaks.*)

ACT II

Scene 2

Harry and Cynthia alone.

CYNTHIA: Harry—the simple life? You blew it.

HARRY. Blew it? I thought I did pretty well. Have you ever seen a Swedish Modern Corral before?

CYNTHIA. But it's not *simple*.

HARRY. It's as simple as I could make it under the circumstances . . . Nobody crosses the Welcome Wagon Vigilantes.

CYNTHIA. I know, darling—I know the pressures you've been going through—from me as well as everyone else.

HARRY. I tried.

CYNTHIA. I know you tried. I know you did the best you could.

HARRY. But it wasn't good enough.

CYNTHIA. I'm so glad you understand.

HARRY. Yeah . . .

CYNTHIA. And you mustn't think I don't appreciate what you've tried to do. I know you've done it for me and I think you're wonderful.

HARRY. Come again?

CYNTHIA. I think you're wonderful and I love you.

HARRY. You what?

CYNTHIA. I love you! I love you! (*Music echoes her words as Harry reacts, then continues under as he speaks.*)

HARRY. You serious?

CYNTHIA. Of course I'm serious you crazy fool. I love you.

HARRY. You don't know how long I've waited to hear you say those words! Oh! Cynthia! . . .

CYNTHIA. Yes, my darling. (*Music out.*)

HARRY. Will you marry me?

CYNTHIA. No.

HARRY. Figures.

CYNTHIA. Harry, I know you'll think I'm irrational, but I can't help it—I have to be that way.

HARRY. You're right.

CYNTHIA. Yes?

36

HARRY. Yes. I think you're irrational.

CYNTHIA. You don't understand. I *do* love you. It's simply that I can't adjust to a man who doesn't *do* anything.

HARRY. OK—Look, Cynthia, I know: You want me to amount to something. But it looks like I'm too rich ever to amount to anything. I don't know what the hell I should do . . . Maybe I should just take all my money and give it away. (*Musical sting. Light-bulb.*)

CYNTHIA. No!

HARRY. Yes! What in the world do I have to offer. Absolutely nothing—except my money. If that's all I have to offer, then I'll offer it—I'll give it to charity!

CYNTHIA. All of it?

HARRY. Of course not.

CYNTHIA. (*Relieved.*) Ohhhh! (*She gets it.*) Oooohhh!!! Harry! —I think you've found it

HARRY. Found it? What?

CYNTHIA. Your perfect vocation—philanthropy! (*Music under.*) Think of the good you'd be doing for others less fortunate than yourself! Yes. Yes! I *could* marry a philanthropist . . . I wouldn't care if he didn't have a penny in the world.

HARRY. Now hold on—are you sure you mean it? I've got to know—because if I blow this, it's the end of the line. I might as well hang-dog it back to East Hampton . . . You mean it?

CYNTHIA. Do I mean it? I do! I do! Oh darling, I think we've finally found your way!

HARRY. This is it? I can have that in writing?

CYNTHIA. This is absolutely it or my name isn't Cynthia Burgess.

HARRY & CYNTHIA. Buxbaum . . .

CYNTHIA. Oh Harry, I'm so happy! Aren't you happy?

HARRY. I sure am!

CYNTHIA. Me too. I'm sure you'll be wonderful at philanthropy —all you have to be is generous and rich, and you're both!

HARRY. I am at that. Maybe you're right, maybe I have found myself at last. C'mon, Cynthia, let's seek out a charitable organization.

CYNTHIA. Do you have your money with you?

HARRY. Only as much as I can afford to lose.

CYNTHIA. Then let's go. I'll be beside you.

HARRY. (*Lifting her up.*) Oh no. You'll be above me! (*They sweep out. Bernie gets up from his table, with drunken dignity. Music out as he speaks.)*

BERNIE. Did you ever hear such noxious twaddle in your life? Y'know, if I didn't love that girl so much, I seriously doubt that I could stand her. I am probably well out of it. I am completely out of it. Hahaha. That's rich. Rich! That's why I can't stand *him* . . . because he is so utterly and absolutely rich, and because he wears those ridiculous white shoes. I hate white shoes. I also hate pointy Italian shoes. And I hate brown paper packages tied up with strings. And I hate every one of you out there, regardless of race, creed, or national origin. *(To piano player, who has been laughing.)* And you shut up. You're no goddamn bed of roses yourself. *(To audience.)* Ladies and gentlemen—I do not want you to gather the impression that I am bitter. I do not want you to think that I am a bad loser. I am a good loser. A very good loser. I am, in fact, a great loser. Perhaps one of the greatest losers of all time —hit it! *(Music. Hat and cane tossed in from offstage. Sings.)*

Give a cheer, give a cheer,
Let me hear it for the loser of the year
If you'd like to learn the secret of my notable success
Grab your notebooks and your pencils while I modestly confess
That it seems to come by instinct, I'm a sort of self-made mess
Give a cheer, for the loser of the year.

Give a cheer, give a cheer,
For the uncontested loser of the year
You can ask my used car dealer if you want to know who's
   smart
Sure of course I bought an Edsel, but hold on, that's just the
   start
You know why I bought an Edsel—'cause my Tucker fell
   apart
Give a cheer—for the loser of the year

Every day I stop myself and tell myself: everything will be
   okay
Every day I stop myself and tell myself: take heart, you'll
   find a way
And while I'm saying this, some guy comes up and tells me
   that

My fly is open
Why am I hopin'
I will never find my way
I have a three year subscription to Colliers . . .
    Give a cheer, give a cheer
    For the undefeated loser of the year
When I was in college, a gambler offered me $500 to throw a
basketball game. But I couldn't make the team.
    Give a cheer, for the loser of the . . .
I went to a bookstore—tried to purchase the complete works of
Frank Lloyd Wright. They sold me sixteen buildings . . . which
I could ill afford.
    Give a cheer, give a cheer
    Give a shout for the outsider of the year
I bought one of those products that offers you double your money
back if not satisfied . . . and I liked it.
    Once I went to see an analyst to learn why I'm a flop
    So he asked for my life story, he said take it from the top
    Well I finally gave up talking when his giggling wouldn't stop.
    Loud and clear—for the loser of the year.
I got arrested for tearing the tag off my mattress.
    Every day I stop myself and tell myself: Everything will be
      okay
    Every day I stop myself and tell myself . . .
I know. You're wondering why I'm going out with a good looking
girl like Cynthia. Well, when I first met her in high school, she
was a real dog—so she got good looking. My luck, right? Right.
Well, I guess it's back to Natalie Hergesheimer—she's a real beast.
Oooops . . . I forgot . . . Natalie Hergesheimer doesn't like me.
My father once offered me $500 to throw a basketball.
There it is—my whole life. I keep waiting and waiting for op-
portunity to knock, and every time I go to the door—it's Avon
calling!
    Give a cheer, give a cheer,
    One more rouser for the loser of the year
    I do everything they tell me to try to get ahead
    I drink mentholated coffee and I smoke the high priced spread
    All my tables are Formica, my clothes are wash and wear
    I used fluoridated toothpaste and I swear by Dial-A-Prayer

But in spite of all my efforts, nobody seems to care
For still they point, call me jerk,
Stone me on my way to work
It's clear . . .
Look, I don't want to take up any more of your time with . . .
(*Stares at his bare wrist.*) Who took my watch?
I'm the loser of the . . .
(*He bumps into arch.*) Aw forget it . . . (*Blackout. Music up on applause.*)

ACT II

Scene 3

Sign appears reading: "The Philanthropist's Progress—A Cautionary Cantata." Music is continuous throughout Scene 3 with cues as indicated in vocal score.

CYNTHIA.
Busy day!
Busy day!
Oh the life of a secretary
I am always so very merry
Busy day!
Busy day!
Ev'ry morning at eight o'clock
I wake up and say "oh, boy"—and stuff like that.
Because I am so happy to be working for my boss—
Mister Mann—who owns many charities—as head of Chari-
    table Institutions, Inc.
Busy day!
Busy day!
I make the coffee and tidy the office,
Type up some letters and things;
Answer the telephone, take some dictation and stuff. How I
    love it!
Busy, busy, busy, busy, busy day!

How I love my work, but how lonely it can become.
How often I have wished that a handsome young man would
    come into my life and carry me away with him—
Far, far away from this charitable work I love so well.
HARRY. (*Entering. Speaks.*) Excuse me, Miss—but is this . . .
(*They stare at each other, spellbound. Sing.*)
HARRY & CYNTHIA.
  I love you!
  I love you! I love you!
  All my life I've searched and dreamed
  How impossible it seemed
  Now suddenly my dreams have all come true—
  And I love you!
(*They kiss.*)
HARRY. (*Spoken.*) No time for this now, Cynthia!
CYNTHIA. (*Spoken.*) Hark! He knows my name!
HARRY. (*Sung.*)
  I have come to see Mister Mann—
  The man who owns these many charities and
  Philanthropic groups.
CYNTHIA. (*Sung.*)
  He is waiting for you in his office.
HARRY.
  He is waiting for me in his office?
  Then to him I will go!

CYNTHIA.	HARRY.
Yes go!	I will go in
Go in and see the boss,	
And when you see him	And make my contribution
Think of me.	To a worthwhile cause.
And I will love you,	
I will love you.	Yes, I will
While I do my chores	Work and slave for
I'll be thinking of you.	Charity—
While I make the coffee,	And widows,
Tidy the office, type some letters;	And undernourished
Answer the telephone,	Orphans,
Take some diction,	And you—

File some papers and stuff—

> I love you!
> I love you!

Busy, busy, busy day!

(*Exits.*)

MAN.

Good morning, sir. Won't you please step in?

Welcome to Charitable Institutions, Inc.

HARRY.

Hiya! My name is Harry Clay and I am very rich.

I have come to donate a million bucks to charity.

MAN.

Accepted with thanks. Ev'ry million counts, you know.

HARRY.

But first would you give me a breakdown of where the money
is to go?

MAN. (*Spoken.*) Of course! (*Sung.*)

15% for operational expenses
25% for miscellaneous
26% for extraneous deductions
6% for overhead
8% for underwear
12% for maintenance
And 10% for other!

HARRY.

Would you mind repeating that?

MAN.	HARRY.
My pleasure!	
15% for operational expenses	
25% for miscellaneous	15%—operational expenses
26% for extraneous deductions	25%—miscellaneous
6% for overhead	26%
8% for underwear	6%
12% for maintenance	8%
And 10% for other!	12%

HARRY.

Wait a minute! That's 102%.

MAN.

Exactly!

(*Spoken.*) You owe us $20,000.

HARRY. (*Sung.*)
I don't understand it! What are these deductions for?
MAN.
15% for operational—
HARRY.
Yes, yes! But where does all that money go?
MAN.
My dear sir, our organization is a vast and expensive proposition.
For we must have our offices, we must have our telephones,
And all those banquets, all that junk mail—and we must pay—
The volunteer mothers.
HARRY.
Do you mean then that none of that money actually goes to the needy?
MAN. (*Spoken.*) Of course not! (*Sung.*)
If we gave our money away to the needy, our organization could not survive, could not remain alive.
(*Spoken.*) And then—we could not perform our charitable work.
HARRY. (*Sung.*)
But that's dishonest!
That's illegal!
What will become of all the groups
That depend on you for . . .
MAN.
Mister Clay, please! Get a hold of yourself!
Remember—our gain is your tax loss.
(*Spoken.*) And besides—beggars can't be choosers, can they?

MAN.	HARRY.
15% for operational expenses	What can I do?
25% for miscellaneous	Have I failed
26% for extraneous deductions	Yet one more time?
6% for overhead	What can I do
8% for underwear	To prove to her——

CYNTHIA. (*Entering.*)
Here are some more checks, Mister Mann.
HARRY & CYNTHIA. (*Transfixed.*)
I love you!
I love you, I love you!

All my life I've searched and
    dreamed
How impossible it seemed
Now suddenly my dreams
    have all come true
 	
And I love you!
	MAN.
	Watching these young people
	List'ning to their song
	
	Hearing their whispered
	    words of love—
	It makes me want to puke!

HARRY. (*Spoken.*) She believes in me! I must do something to renew my faith in myself and be worthy of her— (*Sung.*)

    I have it! I'll start my *own* charity—
    For the widows, and the orphans, and the unhealthy poor.
       I'll go and . . .

MAN.

    Not so fast, my fine young man!
    All philanthropy throughout our land
    Is in the hands of the organization.
    Ev'rything is sewed up and divided
    Neatly into territories,

(*Spoken.*) So don't try to muscle in! (*Sung.*)

    All fatal diseases which have no cure are run by
    Big Stella from St. Louis—
    Don't mess around with her!
    Out in Duluth the seals and the stamps are run by a guy
       known only as "Gramps"
    Nobody crosses him!
    Baltimore Benny runs the envelope game
    And the ladies who shake their cans
    Are under the aegis of someone whose name
    I'm sorry to say is apt to change from day to day—don't get
      in our way!

HARRY.	CYNTHIA.

Nothing you say,
Nothing you do,
Can alter my inflexible course
   —I defy you!
I shall go on my own sweet
   way
And start my own philan-
   thropy
To give to the needy—
	
	Oh, Harry, be careful!
	
	If you get hurt then
	
	What is life for me?

And not to a greedy organization such as this is!		What will become of me? Oh Harry, be careful!
MAN.	HARRY.	CYNTHIA.
No sir! Not a chance, We'll fix your wagon So don't try to take us over.		Oh Harry!
	No sir! You can't scare me off with threats. I'll give to the needy,	You'd be a fool to go! But if you are bound to go
Beware—our trigger man is accurate, He never misses.	And not to a greedy, Grabby, grubby Organization such as this is!	I'll send you on Your own sweet way With love and kisses!
Get out of town! Get out of town! Or you'll find Yourself in danger— Go!		Oh Harry!
	Nothing you say, Nothing you do Can alter my inflexible resolve.	What will become of me?
Get out of town! Get out of town! Get out of town!	I won't be bullied! I won't be threatened! I'll beat you down!	Oh Harry, please! Get out of town!

(*Harry exits.*)

MAN. (*Pantomimes picking up telephone. Spoken.*) Hello—St. Louis? Get me Big Stella. Hello, Stella? No, I don't want to be a doctor. Now listen, Stella—

CYNTHIA. (*Aside. Sung.*)
Hark! He is calling Big Stella.
What is he planning to do?

MAN. (*Sung.*)
We're planning to fix his wagon.

CYNTHIA.
They're planning to fix his wagon.
(*Spoken.*) I must go and warn him! (*Sung.*)

45

I'll go and warn my love
And when I warn him ev'rything will be—
Swell: I will save him, I will save him
From this charitable work I love so well!
(*Exits.*)
HARRY. (*Entering.*)
Busy day!
Busy day!
Oh, how wonderful charity is,
I'm as busy as any bee is.
I'll take my money and make contributions,
Shovel it out to the poor.
I'll ask them how do they like it
And they will say stuff.
How I love it
Busy, busy, busy, busy, busy day.

Now to take my money and distribute it to those who most
deserve it—the poor.
Here comes a man down the street
Who is obviously a pauper.
His ragged clothes and shaggy hair give him away.
Away! I must needs go and save him!
(*Man, wearing battered hat, enters.*)
Kind sir, it is my desire
To help you with some charity.
MAN.
What's that you say?
HARRY.
I would like to give you some money.
MAN.
What's wrong with it?
Are you a crank or a counterfeiter?
HARRY.
This is merely charity.
Please accept my—
MAN.
What do you take me for?
Don't try to make a sucker out of me.

HARRY.

But—

MAN.

Where's the hidden microphone?

Where's the hidden camera?

You must be Allen Funt—

Away! And play your silly tricks on someone else!

(*Exits.*)

HARRY.

This failure won't dissuade me

From my worthwhile cause.

Here comes another man

In ragged clothes and shaggy hair.

(*Man enters, wearing red silk bandanna.*)

Kind sir, it is my desire

To help you with some charity.

MAN.

What's a matter you?

You think that I need charity?

I don't need no charity.

I got my pride.

I get my relief checks.

(*Exits.*)

HARRY.

I must go on!

I must go on!

To prove myself worthy of the one who waits for me to prove

me worthy of her hand.

Here comes a poor blind man—

This must be my lucky day!

(*Man enters wearing sunglasses and carrying cane.*)

Kind sir, I come to you in the name of charity.

MAN. (*Spoken.*) No thanks—I gave at the office. (*Exits.*)

HARRY. (*Sung.*)

Oh have I failed again?

No! I'll go on with my journey.

For what is life to me

If I cannot prove my love to her

And give away my money—and ev'rything—or something.

This man is my last chance.
If he refuses me then I have lost my self-respect—
And Cynthia—and a lot of precious time.
(*Enter Bernie wearing trenchcoat and slouch hat with brim pulled down.*)
Good sir, I am offering you some money.
BERNIE.
Oh sir, I thank you.
HARRY. (*Spoken.*) You mean you'll take it?
BERNIE. (*Spoken.*) Sure I will, buddy.
HARRY.
Jubilation!
This generous deed will be proof enough or I'll be damned!

HARRY.	CYNTHIA. (*Entering.*)
	Harry! They're going to fix your wagon!
	I came as quickly as I could.
I love you!	I must warn you.
I love you! I love you!	I love you! I love you!

BERNIE. (*Spoken.*) Hey, buddy!

HARRY.		CYNTHIA.
All my life I've searched and dreamed.		All my life I've searched and dreamed.

HARRY.	BERNIE.	CYNTHIA.
		Harry! You must listen to me!
How impossible it seemed	Hey, buddy	How impossible it seemed They're going to fix your wagon.
Now suddenly My dreams have all come true. Here—take this with my thanks. (*Gives him money.*) And I love—	(*Turns coat lapel out revealing police badge.*) You're under arrest!	Now suddenly My dreams have all come true. And I love—

HARRY.
Under arrest?
What is the charge?

BERNIE. (*Taking out pad and pencil.*)
    Distributing charity without a license.
(*Enter Mr. Mann wearing hat, neckerchief, sunglasses and carrying cane.*)
    If this kind gentleman hadn't warned me
(*Mr. Mann removes hat, neckerchief, sunglasses.*)
    I might not have been in time
    To prevent this hideous crime
CYNTHIA & HARRY. (*Spoken.*) Mister Mann!
MAN. (*Sung.*)
    Yes, Mister Mann!
    Of course, Mister Mann!
    The syndicate works in mysterious ways
    Its wonders to perform.
CYNTHIA.
    Oh Harry, this is terrible!
    They can't do this to you!
HARRY. (*Spoken.*) You're right Cynthia—It *is* terrible.

HARRY.	CYNTHIA.
To this I've come.	
I have suffered,	
I have tried.	Oh, Harry,
I did it all for you	You have tried
Just to have you	And I believe in you
By my side.	
All the things that I went thru,	I know you've failed—
	You've failed me and
I've tried to find my way.	momma, too,
Thru all the toil and strife of life	
	But I don't care.
I've made my way.	
But I have failed,	For tho' you've failed,
Yes, I have failed,	Somehow my heart
	Won't stop its beating
I have failed.	

49

BERNIE (left) / MAN (right)

                    Oh no, my heart
                    Won't stop its beating,
And now I want   For if my heart
To be alone with   Stopped its beating
All my sorrow,   I would die!
And my mis'ry,   I love you!

And my anguish,   I love you!
And you!   I love you!

BERNIE. (*Spoken.*) O.K. fella, let's get moving.
BERNIE. (*Sung.*)   MAN.
                    This is what it comes to

                    When you mess with the
                        syndicate.

                    I agree with liberty.
Just tell it   "Don't tread on me!"
To the judge

You wanna   He's failed—
Knock it off?   I knew he would.
O.K. I charge   No one can get the best of
You with resisting   me.
Arrest. Nobody
Pulls this stuff
With Sergeant Bartok!   Ah—

That's it, buddy,   All those widows,
Keep on moving.   All those orphans,
Quit it with the   All those undernourished
Goddamn singing!   others
Save the "hearts and Would have suffered
Flowers" for judge! All because of you.

HARRY. (*Throwing money at Bernie and Mr. Mann. Spoken.*)
Here, take this! I don't need it any more!
BERNIE. (*Spoken.*) That's another charge—attempting to bribe
an officer.
CYNTHIA. (*Spoken.*) Oh Harry, they can't do this to you—not
after I've searched and dreamed.

MAN. (Picking up money. Sung.)	CYNTHIA. (Spoken.)	BERNIE. (Sung.)
15% for operational expenses,		
		15 days
25% for miscellaneous,	Something must be	For unlicensed
26% for extraneous de-ductions,	done. Attention must be paid! I'll write	charity
		25 days
6% for overhead,	the New Republic!	For resisting
8% for underwear—	I'll write CORE! I'll	arrest
	call my mother!	And 26 more days
		For bribing an
		officer.

HARRY.	CYNTHIA.	BERNIE.	MAN.
Take me away!	Busy, busy, busy, busy, busy day!	We'll make you pay!	Take him away!

(Blackout.)

ACT II

SCENE 4

Bump lights to full. Harry and Cynthia alone.

HARRY. Well, the trial wasn't so bad, and it was interesting meeting your mother. I didn't know she was a judge. Only I wish she'd stop calling me "doctor."

CYNTHIA. Let her have her dream.

HARRY. Well I'm free. You know, it's funny—here we are exactly where we were when we first met. I'm still a rich guy who does nothing all day long, and you—you're still you.

CYNTHIA. You're wrong, Harry.

HARRY. I'm wrong? You mean you're *not* you?

CYNTHIA. I mean *you're* not *you*. Don't you see, Harry? You've tried everything you could possibly try and you failed.

HARRY. No I haven't.

CYNTHIA. You failed miserably.

HARRY. I did not fail, Cynthia. It wasn't my fault. I couldn't help it.

51

CYNTHIA. Yes it was your fault, Harry. You've made a complete mess out of everything you tried.

HARRY. I haven't made a mess of anything. The system was against me, that's all.

CYNTHIA. You're a failure, Harry. An absolute and complete failure.

HARRY. I am not!

CYNTHIA. You are so!

HARRY. I don't care. I love you. Will you marry me?

CYNTHIA. Yes!

HARRY. Why not?

CYNTHIA. Darling, I said yes.

HARRY. Do you mean it? Oh Cynthia!

CYNTHIA. I can marry a man who's a failure, Harry. That kind of man needs me. I can stay with him always and help him.

BERNIE. (*Entering.*) What about me? I'm a failure.

CYNTHIA. Not a failure, Bernie—a loser.

BERNIE. Uh huh. (*Exits.*)

HARRY. Cynthia, we're going to be so happy.

CYNTHIA. I know we are, dear.

HARRY. And if you like, we won't touch a single penny of my money.

CYNTHIA. Darling, we will touch every single penny of it. (*Music. Bernie and man [as waiter] enter. Man has tray and 4 glasses of champagne which he distributes.*)

ALL. (*Sing.*)
  Thank God we don't have to work for a living
  This shining world is our valentine
  Let's all in chorus express thanksgiving
  Our father pulled his stocks out in '29

  And so we stand where avarice can't touch us
  Safe from the clutches of fearful greed

  Thank God we don't have to work for a living
  Our father did and now we have all we need

  Who wants to work
  When skies are sunny

52

Who wants to work
Who needs the money
We'd rather play
Jack is no dull fellow
We'll rest our cares away
Who wants to work

Who wants to slave
And live for pay day
Why should we save
We're in our hey-day
With time to spare
Space to laze around in
Oh what a life we'll share
Who wants to work

You won't see me, my friend, get caught for speeding
I'll take it slow, I'll take it free
I might sit down and spend some time just reading
Or simply thinking of no one but me

Who needs the strife
And aggravation
Let's make our life
One long vacation
Go with the breeze
Every day is Sunday
Let's take it at our ease
So grab a pair of skis
We'll meet you at the Pyrenees
Who wants to work

So let's relax
Relax together
Lie on our backs
And dig the weather
We'll sit around
Just compound our pleasure

Oh what a life we've found
We'll loaf the clock around
While others founder we'll just smirk
Who wants to work

CURTAIN

PROP LIST*

ACT I

Scene 1:
   Wads and wads of fake money (Harry. Used throughout show)
   Flowers (Mann)
   Fur coat (Mann. Cynthia's size)
   Sandwich on plate (Mann)
   Small American flag (Mann)
   Sparkler (Mann)
   Telephone (Mann)

Scene 2:
   Clipboard (Mann)
   Pencil (Mann)
   Watch (Bernie)
   3 "strike" signs as per script

Scene 3:
   Telephone (Cynthia)

Scene 4:
   Watch (Cynthia)

Scene 6:
   Eyeglasses (Mann)
   Loaded water pistol (Bernie)

Scene 7:
   Telephone (Mann)

ACT II

Scene 1:
   2 cutout pieces of cactus, one turned backwards.
   On it is painted "$—SCENE 8"

*NOTE: Some of these properties may not be available in your area.
         If such is the case, don't do the show.

Scene 2:
   Cane (Bernie)
   Straw hat (Bernie)

Scene 3:
   Cane (Mann)
   Sunglasses (Mann)
   Police badge (Bernie)
   Small pad and pencil (Bernie)

Scene 4:
   Waiter's tray (Mann)
   4 Champagne glasses (Mann)

COSTUME PLOT

The four characters wear the following basic costumes throughout, unless otherwise indicated:

Harry—blue blazer, grey slacks, regimental stripe tie, very new white tennis shoes

Cynthia—simple black cocktail dress

Bernie—plain business suit

Mr. Mann—black business suit w/matching vest

ACT I

Scene 1:

Mr. Mann—tuxedo dickey overdress

Scene 2:

Mr. Mann—change to leather jacket for strike sequence

Scene 4:

Cynthia—white nurse's cap and collar

Mr. Mann—vest and shirtsleeves; surgical cap

Harry—shirtsleeves; surgical cap

Bernie—surgical cap

Scene 6:

Mr. Mann—American Legion cap; pork pie hat; lady's flowered hat; Mickey Mouse Ears

Scene 7:

Mr. Mann—tuxedo dickey overdress

ACT II

Scene 1:

Harry—stylish western hat; neckerchief; vest

Mr. Mann—western hat; shirt; string tie

Bernie—black western hat; black vest; black kerchief

Scene 2:

Bernie—straw hat

Scene 3:

Cynthia—business collar; small white hair bow

Mr. Mann—battered hat; red bandanna

Bernie—trench coat; slouch hat

Scene 4:

Mr. Mann—tuxedo dickey overdress

New
TITLES

A TEXAS TRILOGY:
 THE LAST MEETING OF THE KNIGHTS
  OF THE WHITE MAGNOLIA
 LU ANN HAMPTON LAVERTY
  OBERLANDER
 THE OLDEST LIVING GRADUATE

THE CHERRY ORCHARD

THE ECCENTRICITIES OF A
 NIGHTINGALE

HOLY GHOSTS

PATRICK HENRY LAKE LIQUORS

THE IDIOTS KARAMAZOV

HOPSCOTCH & THE 75TH

RIGHTING

AUTO-DESTRUCT & THE RHESUS
 UMBRELLA

• *Write for Information*

DRAMATISTS PLAY SERVICE, INC.
440 Park Avenue South   New York, N.Y. 10016

New

PLAYS

THE 5TH OF JULY

LANDSCAPE OF THE BODY

THE NIGHT OF THE TRIBADES

OLD MAN JOSEPH AND HIS FAMILY

ULYSSES IN TRACTION

THE MANDRAKE

HOOTERS

THE WAYSIDE MOTOR INN

COUNTING THE WAYS & LISTENING

PATIO/PORCH

AH, EURYDICE!

Inquiries Invited

DRAMATISTS PLAY SERVICE, INC.

440 Park Avenue South   New York, N. Y. 10016